THE PERFECT

ASSIGNMENT

W. J. Scott

COPYRIGHT

Author: W. J. Scott

Second edition released 2016 by Felix
Publishing
2016 e-book release:
ISBN: 978-0-9945755-0-0
2016 paperback release:
ISBN: 978-0-9945755-7-9

2015 e-book release:
ISBN: 978-0-9871442-4-9
2015 paperback release:
ISBN: 978-0-9871442-5-6
First released in 2015 by Rico Bruesch
Publishing

Registration:
Thorpe-Bowker
Level 1, 607 St Kilda Road
Melbourne, VIC 3000, Australia
tel: +61 3 8517 8342
e-mail: bowkerlink@thorpe.com.au

OTHER BOOKS IN THIS SERIES

MAKE LIFE SIMPLER

by W.J.Scott

The Perfect Assignment
ISBN: 978-0-9945755-0-0

Debt Free, The Morals of Money
Management,

How to Live Within Your Means
and Be Happy
ISBN: 978-0-9945755-2-4

Libre de Deuda, de la moral de la
administración del dinero
ISBN: 978-0-9945755-1-7

Swift, Simple, Sweet!
ISBN: 978-0-9945755-3-1

All books available in digital versions through the usual channels and print versions by contacting the publisher

info@felixpublishing.com

FELIX
PUBLISHING

ABOUT THE AUTHOR

W. J. SCOTT

Wendy holds a Dip. Teach Sec. Sc., and since 1988 has taught teenagers to enjoy Science. Later she went on to acquire a B.Ed., (not the thing you sleep on) in counselling and religious education. More recently, Wendy undertook studies in financial planning, which she then upgraded to an advanced financial planning diploma. Recently she completed studies in a master of teaching English as a foreign language. She was granted membership to the Australian College of Education, and the Doll Artisan Guild. Wendy is also an advanced First Aid instructor with St John, and qualified to teach safe driving for the Road Safety Council.

Among her other interests: Wendy also plays the organ at church; is a Neighbourhood Watch block coordinator; and has won the Ryan Award for community service.

10% of the royalties that she receives from this book, before tax, will be split as donations between World Vision, Fred Hollows Foundation and the Salvation Army.

CONTENTS

PREPARATION

1.   Read the instructions thoroughly.

2.   Read   the   instructions   again,
carefully, and do not assume anything.

3.   Read the instructions thoroughly
once   more,   but   this   time   use   a
highlighter to note all the things that
must be included, and all the choices
you have.

DO NOT PANIC! 30 MINUTES MAX.

4.   Make sure that you have done
steps 1 to 3 inclusive properly, then
choose from the given choices, the
topic that interests and inspires you, the
one you are passionate about and that

you will research thoroughly. An assignment is about your ability to do research, analyse the information, and form it into new ideas and points of view.

10 MINUTES MAX

5. Never use Wikipedia as a source of information in any assignment, for any reason. Consider Wikipedia suitable only for recreation and curiosity, like red cordial which is supposed to be drunk sparingly and not called food.

6. Planning
   a. Select a very broad topic
   b. Select 5 major parts of that topic on which to do research
   c. Select from 3 to 5 parts of each of these subtopics

d. Have 7 sheets of scrap paper (one for each subtopic, or two in case you change your mind), two biros, high lighter, scissors, photocopy funds, library card, and assignment sheet.

Page setup should consist of:

a. 2-2.5cm indent;

b. 12 Ariel for text;

c. Use bold only for headings, not for emphasis.

d. Double line spacing;

e. One space after commas;

f. Two spaces after a full stop or colon;

g. Do not indent paragraphs, or do an extra space;

h. Use double justified format, with header including your name, date and title, as well as page number.

This saves lost pages and others "borrowing" your assignment;

i. Prepare to hand in at least a week early, it saves last minute problems, and allows for all sorts of mishaps like printer breakdown, library closed that morning etc. This saves stress and makes you look as good as you are; and

j. Start on the assignment as soon as you have all the knowledge to do it.

RESEARCH

Before you start, if you are good at Maths and Sciences, draw out a graphic outline to guide your research with each subtopic on a separate page, leaving spaces under each sub subtopic for notes and quotes. If you are better at the Arts, just do a page for each subtopic and put random ideas in bubbles to draw together later. Do what works for you.

Go to the library first, before you go online. **ALLOW 2 HOURS** for a thorough job.

For a 2000 word assignment you need at least 2 books, 2 journals, and 2 URLs (web sites), for a decent grade. But, if you are aiming for A+ you will need 3 books, 3 journals and 3 URLs.

Books usually contain tried and tested research and are heavily reviewed, because of this, their information could be a few years older, though more likely valid. The journals contain up to date, current research. Choose well known and respected journals for your subject, for example 'New Scientist' rather than 'Dolly'. The journals in school and university libraries have been carefully selected for this purpose. When choosing URLs, look at who is producing them, their credentials, and how recently they have been updated. URLs that are part of an .org domain usually contain more professional opinions as they are produced by registered organisations in their field. URLs that are part of a .edu domain are more academic and usually contain doctoral and research theses. URLs that end in .com or .net contain the least credible information as they can be registered by anyone and there is no guarantee that statements are accurate. They will usually contain biased and commercial viewpoints. Make sure you have divergent views in your resources.

You need to compare and contrast these views to form your own ideas. First look up the journals for articles on your main topics, then sub-topics. If the article is 3 pages or less, copy the pages and photocopy the title page for your bibliography. Then staple the pages together, before looking at the next article. Next, you go to the master index and look up your topic, note down the Dewey number and a couple of titles. Then go to that section of the bookcase, open to the table of contents in the first book that takes your fancy. Does it have a chapter on your subtopics? If yes, then flick to it and skim read to find some useful information. If you find anything useful, photocopy pages of quotes along with title page information, then staple it. Continue in this manner until you have gathered information on each subtopic. Use at least 3 different books, with one to three quotes from each book.

Now follow the same procedure with the journals. Instead of just photocopying the page, copy the whole article, most journal articles are only 1-5 pages long and you may find that there is more useful information once you have read further and know more. Make sure you note on the articles the volume and issue numbers as well as the date and the journal from which it is taken. The best journals are always in the libraries, New Scientist, Nature, Scientific American are the best for science, Business Review Weekly, Harvard Business Review, The New

Economist, and the Financial Review are best for business. Check with the teacher or lecturer which journals they recommend. A good indicator is to check out the ones used in class notes and in the text books.

After locating other sources make sure your prescribed text is quoted as well to prove that you have opened it!

Before you put the books and journals back, using pen and in one or two words write the topic of your quote, then highlight it on the photocopy. Return the books and journals when you are sure you have all the bibliography details, either stapled to the quote or written on it. Put all the photocopies and assignment sheet in the one folder. If you have multiple quotes from the one book, and it has excellent background information, use scrap paper torn up to mark the pages, with detail written on the paper, and borrow the book. Check first with the teacher whether pictures are appropriate, mostly not, but if encouraged, internet is your friend.

Now you can go on to the internet. You have now read enough to understand what you are reading on the net. Search by subtopic, choose your site by quality, relevance, author, and recency, print the pages including author details, write down date and time of access with the URLs. On each stapled printout, write the subtopic and highlight the quotes. Put this in the folder. Do not have more than 4 internet sites unless you have more than 4 books and 4 journals, balance is important.

THE TITLE PAGE

Note your title page is centred, in bold text, in a font which is easy to read. For Sciences and Maths assignments you should use Arial font, but other fonts may be permitted for Arts assignments so long as they are legible.

TITLE PAGE DETAILS

YOUR SUBTOPIC

YOUR NAME
(OTHERS IN YOUR GROUP IF NECESSARY)

SUBJECT

YEAR LEVEL

TEACHER

DUE DATE

CERTIFICATION:
I certify the content of this assignment to be my own and original work, and that all sources have been accurately reported and acknowledged. This document has not previously been submitted in part or in its entirety at any educational establishment.

NOW shuffle your photocopies and printouts into alphabetical order by author.

Write your Bibliography (a.k.a. References) using your computer. Use the Harvard system unless told otherwise. If you have a recent version of Word with references on the toolbar, use it. After setting it to the appropriate referencing, it will simplify everything for you. You just enter the data and it takes care of bibliography and makes citing simple. I have included a more detailed section on referencing in the Appendix, but the main types are listed below.

Plagiarism is using another author's ideas, observations or theories and presenting them as your own. This can be as simple as directly copying a single sentence or part of a sentence without quotations (citations) and failing to state its source. Plagiarism is a form of cheating and will result in a failure mark for your assignment. This can sometimes lead to exclusion from school or the course as well.

Collusion is when students who are working together in groups are sharing ideas. If assignments are to be submitted individually then collusion is also a form of cheating and will result in a failure mark. This does not apply to assignments that are to be submitted together as a group, in which case each group member's name must appear on the assignment's title page. This is taken very seriously, do not share or help your friends by letting them see your work for this reason, you will both be penalised.

BIBLIOGRAPHY

BROWN, A.B., 2010, *The Feral Cat Problem,* Letters to the Editor, The Courier Mail, Brisbane, 30 May 2011.

Department of the Environment. (2014). *Feral Cats.* Available: http://www.environment.gov.au/biodiversity/invasive-species/feral-cats. Last accessed 24 June 2015.

JONES, A.B., 2011, *The Feral Cat Problem*, Letters to the Editor, The Courier Mail, Brisbane, 30 May 2011.

SCOTT, W.J., 2015 *The Perfect Assignment,* Felix Publishing, Brisbane.

Now create the title page with all the relevant details as per my front page. An assignment must have an introduction that introduces all the topics answered in the conclusion.

Write the introduction last, after you have done the rest of your assignment, and just slip it in at the beginning, that way it allows you to diverge with extra reading.

STYLE

Write in past tense impersonal. Do not write I saw a dog. Instead, write "a dog was seen."

For every comment back it up with your quotes and research. If you are using a direct quote of one phrase put it in quotation marks and state that someone said it.

Scott, 2011 stated "a dog was seen"

A longer quote, such as a sentence or more, needs to be indented with smaller print. Note this should only be used occasionally and it is not included in word count.

Scott, 2011 stated:

A dog was seen near the fire hydrant on the corner of Tramway Road and Samford Road last week.

To compare and contrast, this way is preferred:

Scott, 2011 stated that she had seen a dog, however Jones, 2011 thought it might have been a large cat. Large feral cats have been seen in this area by both Brown, 2010, and Smith 2010. The Department of the Environment 2014 is concerned at the effect on native species of the feral cats and considers this a major environmental problem. Brown 2010 suggests that……., also works well if you have summarised someone's writings.

Do not use slang, colloquialisms, abbreviations, swear words or insulting language. If you are using a spell checker make sure it is set to Australian or UK English, not American (US English). Make sure the grammar is correct. Get an older adult to read it for accuracy. Older adults tend to recognise spelling and grammatical errors easily (the ones that were brought up before spell checker are best, they actually had to learn the rules).

Now you use your computer to organize and prepare.

Use one or two words for each of the topics and subtopics. You should have decided which sub parts are most significant, and those about which you can find discussions in books, journals, and on the internet. Remember no Wikipedia, not now, not ever! (If you are desperate and really cannot find a valid website related to one of your topics that is not directed at primary school children, yes you can go to Wikipedia. Then, when you visit Wikipedia and find something useful, go to the end of the article, find out who wrote it, and if they are reliable, then look up the original source. Find out more details, and only quote the original source not the wiki!

Now copy the following section from here to..................

Introduction (label it)

Sentence 1 your topic and all the subtopics in order

Sentence 2 subtopic 1

Sentence 3 subtopic 2

Sentence 4 subtopic 3

Sentence 5 subtopic 4

Sentence 6 subtopic 5

Sentence 7 sum up all the
subtopics and lead back to the
first subtopic

Paragraph 1

Sentence 1 subtopic 1 and all
the sub subtopics in order

Sentence 2 sub subtopic 1

Sentence 3 sub subtopic 2

Sentence 4 sub subtopic 3

Sentence 5 sub subtopic 4

Sentence 6 sub subtopic 5

Sentence 7 sum up all the sub subtopics and lead to the
subtopic 2

Paragraph 2

Sentence 1 subtopic 2 and all the sub subtopics in order

Sentence 2 sub subtopic 1

Sentence 3 sub subtopic 2

Sentence 4 sub subtopic 3

Sentence 5 sub subtopic 4

Sentence 6 sub subtopic 5

Sentence 7 sum up all the sub subtopics and lead to the
Subtopic 3.

Paragraph 3

Sentence 1 subtopic 3 and all the sub subtopics in order

Sentence 2 sub subtopic 1

Sentence 3 sub subtopic 2

Sentence 4 sub subtopic 3

Sentence 5 sub subtopic 4

Sentence 6 sub subtopic 5

Sentence 7 sum up all the sub subtopics and lead to the subtopic 4

Continue until all subtopics covered

Conclusion

Sentence 1 your topic and all the subtopics in order

Sentence 2 subtopic 1

Sentence 3 subtopic 2

Sentence 4 subtopic 3

Sentence 5 subtopic 4

Sentence 6 subtopic 5

Sentence 7 sum up all the subtopics, make this a very powerful sentence, and the previous 6 sentences should be compressed.

HERE.........

Now go back to your notes and replace all the words topic and subtopic with your chosen one or two words.

Well done! You have now done all the hard work, the rest is just joining the dots.

Start with paragraph 1 (remove that label)

Look at all you have on those topics, look back at your printed references, this is quicker and easier and less stressful than storing everything on the computer and going back and forth, and it allows you to be in control by shuffling the papers into the right order, you can see all of them at once.

Here is an example:

Assignment: Environmental Impact of Pets

Topic 1:   Dogs

Subtopics: Size of yard
Training
Natural behaviour
Aggression
Hunting
Pollution

Topic 2: Cats

Topic 3: Birds

Topic 4: Pets as helpers

Topic 5: Pet rescue services

Conclusion

Introduction

Abstract – if required

Dogs have significant impact on both the natural and built environment, this can be increased or lessened by the size of the yard, training, natural behaviours, their aggression, hunting instincts and efforts to reduce pollution. A large dog in a small yard tends to be louder and more aggressive according to Abbott, 2013, Brown 2012 states however, that large dogs should never be kept in small suburban yards at all. The natural behaviour of dogs is to live in a pack, their owners need to be the leaders here guiding and directing behaviours (Vet 2012). Should owners fail to provide this training, the natural aggression, according to Crystal, 2012, will be the controlling force. Dawes, 2012, states that hunting native wildlife provides stimulus and extra food for underfed or bored pets. The pollution of footpaths is significant from dogs, this was the reason given by BBC 2000, for imposing a $120 fine for failing to carry a disposal bag or failing to clean up after a dog. This is helping, but the bags themselves are a source of pollution. Whilst training and responsible pet ownership would reduce these impacts with dogs, is the same true for cats?

Note how the subtopics were addressed in order, heavily referenced, started with a summary, and finished with a summary that lead to the next paragraph on cats. This was done by deleting each topic as it was covered.

That done it is easy to follow to the next paragraph comfortably and naturally.

Set up the page numbering at the start with a page number on every page except the coversheet. If it is a long assignment or extended research the same rules follow however a table of contents is appropriate. Ensure that there is a header on each page so individual pages are identified as your work.

Add a statement that this is your own work date and sign it. Never download an assignment even to look at. All teaching staff have access to checkers, such as Turnitin. Never state a comment is your own if it is not.

You can check for plagiarism and originality of your assignment online for free by uploading it to http://paperrater.com/plagiarism_checker.
Make sure you remove your bibliography before uploading your assignment to this website.

Reread the marking scheme for Very High Achievement, and check that you can tick all the boxes. Keep a printed copy at home safely in case it is lost. Keep it in the folder with your research.

Presentation is important, print or electronically send as required. Verify that your assignment has been received in full. Hand it in when the marker is at his/her desk, not when charging out to the next lesson. Make sure your assignment does not contain any dirty hand marks, or dog tooth marks, or coatings of last week's lunch. Use black print on white. It will probably be marked late at night so the marker will need to be able to see the text clearly.

This format is used with minor variations all the way through University. Once you have accepted and are comfortable with the fact that your opinions are not valid unless backed up by others until after your PhD, and it is the research that is important, you will find this easy. Just make sure the format is as stated in the assignment cover sheet. Some use APS rather than Harvard, which is just as easy to set up on your computer.

 If you follow these instructions to the letter then you will certainly get a very high mark. You will understand the topic. Your assignment will be unique. You have proof of your research and have the satisfaction of a job well done. In most cases this would translate into an A+. I have tried it and done an average university level assignment in one day, 6 am to 6 pm, and scored straight A's. When I tried to do it my preferred way, letting them know how much I knew, I did not score well, it was a struggle and took so much longer.

Follow this guide and do it well, and quickly and know what you are doing, or do it your way...

In an examination, if you are required to write an essay, using this method is the quickest way to write a logical, informative and well-structured paper. It should save valuable time and lower stress as you are literally in control. If you should later decide to write a book this format will help you order your thoughts and make it easier to read and understand. The whole idea about style is that it helps you to focus on what is important without leaving anything of importance out.

APPENDIX

HARVARD REFERENCING

Referencing guides are available at:

• University of Tasmania Library 2009, *Referencing and Assignment Writing*: Harvard, online guide, University of Tasmania, viewed 25 February 2009,

http://utas.libguides.com/content.php?pid=27520&sid=199808

• University of Melbourne Library 2010, *Harvard Style general notes, online guide*, University of Melbourne, viewed 3 November 2010,

<http://www.lib.unimelb.edu.au/recite/citations/printableDocs/Harvard%20Style%20General%20Notes.pdf>

You can also use the following URLs to create Harvard Style References for your assignment:

<http://www.neilstoolbox.com/bibliography-creator>

The following summary is sourced from the Style manual for authors, editors and printers 2002, 6th edn, Wiley Australia.

Books (print and online)	
one author	Goldsworthy, J 2010, *Parliamentary sovereignty: contemporary debates*, Cambridge studies in constitutional law, Cambridge University Press, Cambridge.

Books (print and online)	
two or more authors	Flexer, RW, Baer, RM, Luft, P & Simmons, TJ 2008, *Transition planning for secondary students with disabilities*, 3rd edn, Pearson, Upper Saddle River, New Jersey.
edited books	Ahdar, R & Aroney, N (eds) 2010, *Shari'a in the West*, Oxford University Press, Oxford.
part of a series	Muller, R & Turner, JR 2010, *Project-oriented leadership*, Advances in project management, Gower, Farnham, England.
chapters in edited books	Brandt, RB 2002, 'Defective newborns and the morality of termination', in J Arthur (ed.), *Morality and moral controversies: readings in moral, social, and political philosophy*, 6th edn, Prentice Hall, Upper Saddle River, New Jersey, pp. 253-60.
editions	Stewart, A 2009, *Stewart's guide to employment law*, 2nd edn, Federation Press, Annandale, New South Wales.
part of a series	Muller, R & Turner, JR 2010, *Project-oriented leadership*, Advances in project management, Gower, Farnham, England.

Books (print and online)	
anonymous (no author or editor given)	*The stage acquitted: being a full answer to Mr Collier, and other enemies of the drama* 1996, Routledge/Thoemmes, London.
conference proceedings	Zhang, J & Xi, W 2012, 'Optimal nonlinear damping for inelastic structures using dimensional analysis', *20th analysis and computation specialty conference 2012*, proceedings of a meeting sponsored by the American Society of Civil Engineers held 29-31 March, Chicago, Illinois, Curran Associates, Red Hook, New York, pp.97-106.
corporate authors	Department of Energy 1980, *Projections of energy needs*, HMSO, London.
online books	McClain, M & Roth JD 1999, Schaum's quick guide to writing great essays, McGraw-Hill, New York, viewed 17 January 2005, <http:// ezproxy.usq.edu.au/login?url=http:// site.ebrary.com/lib/unisouthernqld/Doc? id=5002145>.
Journals and newspaper articles	
one author	Wong, K 2009, 'Rethinking the hobbits of Indonesia', *Scientific American*, vol. 301, no. 5, pp. 66-73.

Journals and newspaper articles	
two or more authors	Gibberd, R, Snow, PT, Rice, PG & Patel, NB 1991, 'Nuclear power at what price?', *The Bulletin*, vol. 113, June 4, pp. 51-5.
newspaper article	Popham, B 1987, 'Saving the future', *Weekend Australian Magazine*, 7-8 February, p. 10.
online journal article	Griffith, Al 1995, 'Coordinating family and school: mothering for schooling', *Education Policy Analysis Archives*, vol. 3, no. 1, viewed 12 February 1997, <http://olam.ed.asu.edu/epaa/>.
online newspaper article	*Economist* 2014, 'How young is too young, 15 November, viewed 21 November 2014, <http://www.economist.com/news/international/21632522-laws-teenage-sex-are-converging-so-thinking-about-their-purpose-how-young-too>

Online documents and websites	
online document	Australian Taxation Office 2012, *Income tax: deductibility of self-education expenses incurred by an employee or a person in business, taxation ruling*, TR 98/9, Australian Taxation Office, viewed 6 February 2013, <http://law.ato.gov.au/atolaw/view.htm?DocID=TXR/TR989/NAT/ATO/00001&PiT=99991231235958>.
online document (no author)	*Educating America for the 21st century: developing a strategic plan for educational leadership by Columbia University 1993-2000 (initial workshop draft)* 1994, draft workshop report, Institute for Learning Technologies, Columbia University, viewed 16 May 1995, <http://ariel.adgrp.com/~ghb/trips/940717_ICT/policy/ILT/EdPlan.html>.
website	The Body Shop Australia 2003, The Body Shop Australia, Mulgrave, Victoria, viewed 31 January 2003, <http://www.thebodyshop.com.au/>.

Online documents and websites	
online images	AC Nielsen 2008, *Consumer confidence, concerns, spending and attitudes to recession: a global Nielsen consumer report*, digital image, AC Nielsen, viewed 21 August 2008, <http://au.acnielsen.com/site/documents/GlobalNielsenConsConfConcReportJune08b.pdf>.
online data sets	Bureau of Meteorology 2011, *High-quality Australian daily rainfall dataset*, Australia's high-quality climate change datasets, data file, Australian Government, Bureau of Meteorology, viewed 17 November 2011, <ftp://ftp.bom.gov.au/anon/home/ncc/www/change/HQdailyR>.
Microform, patents, standards and maps	
microform	Herbert, WG 1987, *The Australian beef industry: an overview*, Australian Livestock Council, Canberra, microfiche.
patent	Connor, PM 2005, *Collector for solar radiation*, Australian Patent 2004243336.

Microform, patents, standards and maps	
standard	International Organization for Standardization 2003, *Traveller irrigation machines - part 1 - operational characteristics and laboratory and field test methods*, ISO 8224-1:2003, International Organization for Standardization, Geneva.
online standards	Standards Australia 2003, *Installation of security screen doors and window grilles*, AS 5040-2003, Standards Australia, Sydney, viewed 16 September 2008, <http://www.saiglobal.com/online/autologin.asp>.
maps	Department of Mines and Energy 2007, *Queensland gold resources*, Australia 1:3 000 000 geological series, sheet 9986, Department of Mines and Energy, Brisbane, Queensland.
online maps	*Logan Central QLD* 2010, street map, Google maps, Australia, viewed 10 August 2010, <http://maps.google.com.au/maps?h1=en&tab=w1>.

Audiovisual examples	
DVD	*Fahrenheit 9/11* 2004, DVD, Columbia TriStar Home Entertainment, Culver City, California. Written, produced and directed by Michael Moore.
video	*Grumpy meets the orchestra* 1992, video recording, Australian Broadcasting Corporation, Sydney. Featuring the Sydney Symphony Orchestra.
motion picture (film)	*Sunday too far away* 1975, motion picture, South Australian Film Corporation, Adelaide. Distributed by Rainbow Products Ltd, Sydney, and starring Jack Thompson, Reg Lye and Max Cullen.
television program	*What are we going to do with the money?* 1997, television program, ABC Television, Sydney, 8 August.

Audiovisual examples	
radio program	*The search for meaning* 1998, radio program, ABC Radio, Sydney, 24 March.
CD-ROM	*Australia through time* 1994, CD-ROM, Random ROM in assoc. with the ABC, Sydney.
Legislation and legal authorities (for use in-text citations only, not included in bibliography)	
acts	*Anti-Discrimination Act 1991* (Qld)
bills	Anti-terrorism Bill 2004 (House of Representatives)
legal authorities (cases)	*The Commonwealth v. The State of Tasmania* (1983) 158 CLR 1; (1983) 57 ALJR 450; (1983) 46 ALR 625 (the *Tasmanian Dam Case*)
Unpublished works	
theses, papers and abstracts	Langdon, WB 1996, 'Data structures and genetic programming', PhD thesis, University College, London.

Unpublished works	
manuscripts	Benton, TH 1847, 'Letter to Charles Fremont, 22 June', John Charles Fremont Papers, Southwest Museum Library, Los Angeles.